I am Muslim

Cath Senker

Photography by Jenny Matthews

W
FRANKLIN WATTS
LONDON • SYDNEY

© 2005 Franklin Watts

First published in 2005
by Franklin Watts
96 Leonard Street
London
EC2A 4XD

Franklin Watts Australia
45-51 Huntley Street
Alexandria
NSW 2015

Acknowledgements
The author and publishers would like to thank the following for all their help
in the production of this book: Bashir, Saira, Mariyam, Hafsah, Saffiyah,
Aaliyah and Hana Sattar; Rukiya Bai Sattar; Imam Abdul Aziz of Finchley
Islamic Centre, Warda Seliem, Abdul Kader Ellam, Yusuf Ghalayini.

The photos on pages 19, 26-7 were kindly provided by the Sattar family.

Note: When Muslims say the name of one of the prophets, they always say
'Peace Be Upon Him' afterwards, which is shown in this book as 'pbuh'.

Photographer Jenny Matthews
Designer Steve Prosser
Series editor Adrian Cole
Art Director Jonathan Hair
Consultant Ghulam Sarwar,
Muslim Educational Trust

ISBN 0 7496 5931 9

Dewey Classification: 297

A CIP catalogue record for this book is available from the British Library.

Printed in China

Contents

All about me

My name's Aaliyah. I'm 8 years old and I'm a Muslim. Muslims are followers of **Islam**.

At school my favourite subject is English. I also like running and tennis.

At home I enjoy using the computer. I also like playing with my sisters, Saffiyah and Hana (they're 10 and 6).

My family

Saffiyah, Hana and I live with Mum and Dad in London. My eldest sisters, Mariyam and Hafsah, go to an Islamic **boarding school**.

'We live as British people, but with Muslim beliefs.' Aaliyah's Dad

Dad's a businessman, and Mum looks after us and our home. Our family comes from Pakistan, but we have lots of relatives nearby - including Nan.

It's fun helping Mum. We are making chapatis (flat bread).

My Muslim beliefs

We believe in one God, Allah. Allah spoke through his messenger, the **Prophet Muhammad** (pbuh), and his messages were written down to form the **Qur'an**.

We follow our faith by praying, **fasting** at **Ramadan** and giving money to charity. Once in our lifetime, we hope to go to the holy city of **Makkah**.

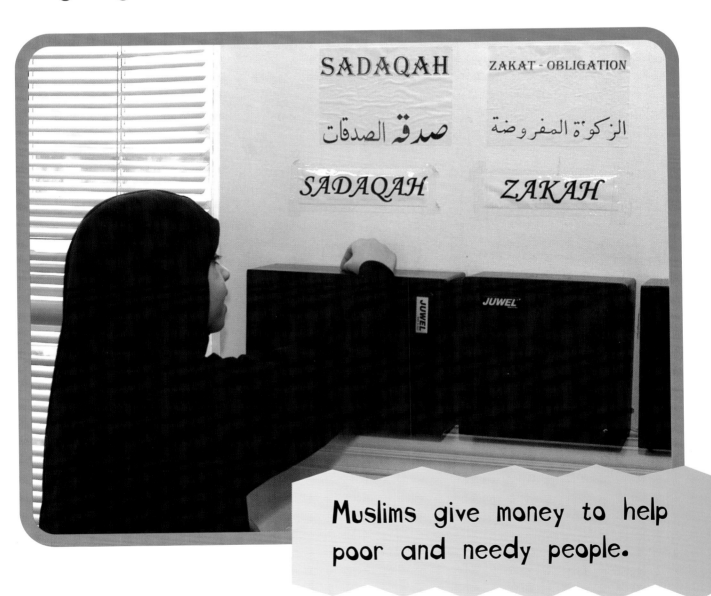

Muslims give money to help poor and needy people.

Worship at home

Muslims pray five times every day. I say prayers with Mum, Saffiyah and Hana.

Before I pray, I wash in the proper way and put on my headscarf, called a **hijab**. I lay out my prayer mat.

I raise my hands to my ears and say Allahu Akbar, which means Allah is great.

When we pray, we face towards the Holy Ka'bah, which is in Makkah, Saudi Arabia.

During the prayers we bow down to Allah.

13

Our clothes

The Qur'an says that hair is part of a woman's beauty, so women should cover their heads in public. I wear a cloak, called a **burka**, and my hijab to go to the mosque.

Mum and my eldest sisters always wear a hijab when they go out. When I'm older, I will too.

Dad wears a long white robe and prayer hat for worship.

Our food

Muslims don't eat animals that feed on other animals. We never eat meat from pigs. Our meat is called **halal**. It comes from animals that are killed in a special way.

We mostly eat Pakistani food at home.

My favourite foods are samosas (right), spaghetti and yuchni (a rice dish).

During Ramadan, we fast. We don't eat or drink between sunrise and sunset.

We break our fast during Ramadan with some dates and water.

At the mosque

The mosque is where Muslims worship, study Islam and hold social events.

Women and girls don't usually go to prayers at the mosque. We go to religion classes and events.

On Fridays, Dad goes to the mosque with the other men for midday prayers.

Everyone takes off their shoes before entering the mosque.

The **imam** gives a talk based on verses from the Qur'an, or a story about the Prophet Muhammad (pbuh). The worshippers then say prayers together.

The Muezzin is the man who calls Muslims to prayer at the mosque.

The imam

Our religious teacher is Imam Abdul Aziz. He leads prayers at the mosque and visits old and sick people in our community.

The imam (left) is speaking to one of the elders of our community.

The imam carries out Muslim ceremonies, such as weddings and funerals.

We ask our imam questions about Islamic teaching. He also gives advice on dealing with problems in an Islamic way.

The Qur'an

The Qur'an is written in beautiful Arabic poetry.

The Qur'an contains the words of Allah. It guides us in all aspects of our lives.

In my favourite story from the Qur'an, the Prophet Abraham (pbuh) has a dream. He is asked to **sacrifice** his only son, Isma'il. Abraham (pbuh) prepares to sacrifice his son, but Allah provides a ram to sacrifice instead. This was a test of his faith in Allah.

You can see verses from the Qur'an around the mosque.

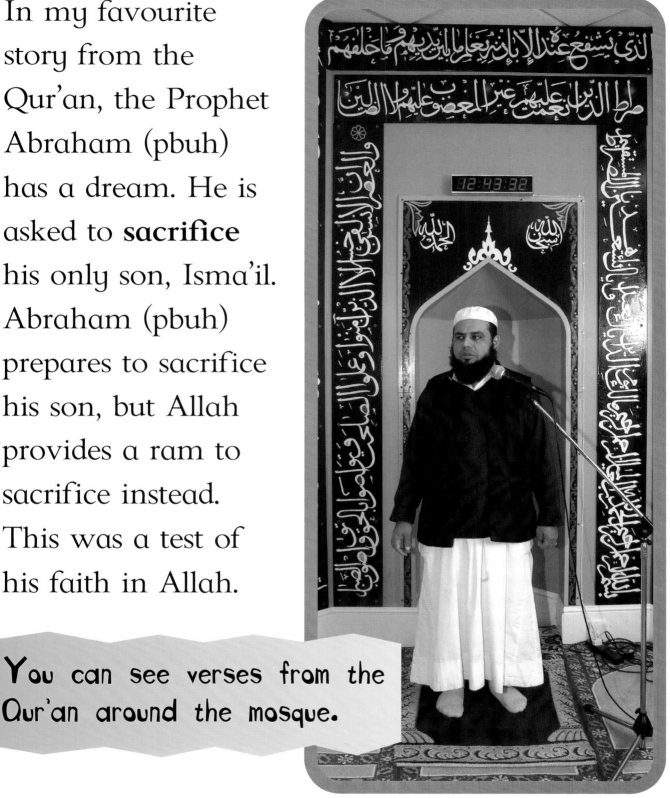

Learning about Islam

I mainly learn about being a Muslim at home, but my sisters and I also attend religion classes. We study the Qur'an and learn about the teachings of Islam.

Saffiyah and I have already read all of the Qur'an. Now we're going to advanced classes to learn about the meaning of the Qur'an.

'I make sure the children understand the meaning of the prayer rituals.'
Warda, Qur'an teacher.

My favourite festival

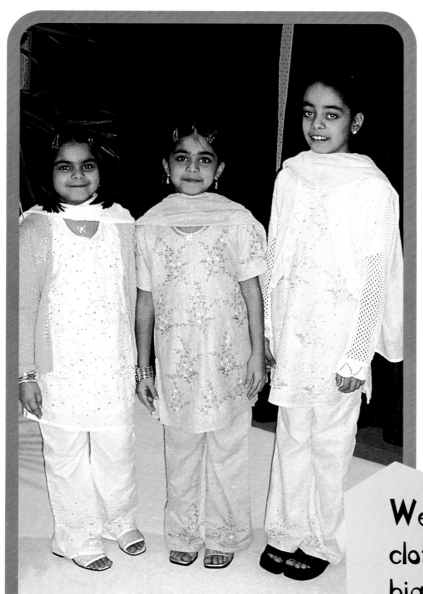

My favourite festival is Id-ul-Adha, the biggest Muslim festival. We celebrate Abraham's sacrifice (pbuh) - see pages 22-3.

We dress up in new clothes for the biggest Muslim festival of the year.

Id is brilliant because my family gets together.
After Id prayers Dad arranges Qurbani.

We eat meat at the feast of Id-ul-Adha.

Qurbani is when a ram is sacrificed in
the name of Allah. We give the meat
to our family, friends and the poor.

Glossary

boarding school
A school where the children stay for the whole term. They come home in the holidays.

burka
A long, black cloak that covers the whole body except for the face.

fasting
Going without food and water for religious reasons.

halal
Specially prepared meat.

hijab
A headscarf that Muslim women and girls wear to cover their hair.

Islam
The religion that Muslims follow.

imam
A Muslim leader.

Makkah
The holy city in modern-day Saudi Arabia where the Prophet Muhammad (pbuh) was born and where he started to teach his message.

Prophet Muhammad (pbuh)
According to Muslims, the final prophet sent by Allah to teach people how to live a good life and worship him. He lived in the sixth century CE.

Qur'an
The Muslim holy book, written in 114 chapters called surahs.

Ramadan
The Muslim month during which Muslims do not eat or drink between sunrise and sunset.

sacrifice
To kill something to offer to Allah.

Websites

http://atschool.eduweb.co.uk/carolrb/islam/islamintro.html
Information for primary school children about customs, the Prophet Muhammad (pbuh), the Qur'an, festivals, daily life, mosques and Islamic art.

www.bbc.co.uk/religion/religions/islam/index.shtml
Muslim history, customs, beliefs, worship and holy days.

www.hitchams.suffolk.sch.uk/mosque/default.htm
All about the Jamia mosque in Derby.

www.reonline.org.uk/shells/strath_iafacts.html
Various Islamic artefacts are explained with photos.

www.submission.org/YES/child2.html
A Muslim site about Ramadan, with activities for children.

http://website.lineone.net/~jlancs/Islam.htm
Frenchwood primary school site, with information about prayer, the mosque, clothes, festivals, Ramadan and weddings.

Note to parents and teachers
Every effort has been made by the Publishers to ensure that these websites are suitable for children; that they are of the highest educational value, and that they contain no inappropriate or offensive material. However, because of the nature of the Internet, it is impossible to guarantee that the contents of these sites will not be altered. We strongly advise that Internet access is supervised by a responsible adult.

Index